PINNACLES
GUIDE

Pinnacles National Monument
San Benito County, California

by

Elvin R. Johnson & Richard P. Cordone

Tillicum Press

1994

Second Edition

Tillicum Press
P.O. Box 1174
Stanwood, WA 98292

Pinnacles Guide
Pinnacles National Monument
San Benito County, California

ISBN 0-9643492-0-5

By Elvin R. Johnson and Richard P. Cordone

TABLE OF CONTENTS

Cover: *High Peaks from Chaparral*

ACKNOWLEDGMENTS

Many people have helped the authors compile this booklet and we thank them. We do not have space to name them all, but the contributions of a few have been invaluable.

Steve DeBenedetti, Resource Management Specialist, brought us up-to-date with information regarding prescribed burning, rock climbing management and feral pig problems.

We are indebted to Kathy Williams, Park Ranger and Interpretive Specialist, for her thorough critique and suggestions for improving this second edition of Pinnacles Guide.

Old friend, C.M. "K" Molenaar, leading geologist with the USGS, took the time to review the complete manuscript for technical wording as well as suggestions regarding the geology and natural history.

Park Superintendent James Sleznick, Jr., spent several hours with us discussing many aspects of the monument, from future plans to maintenance and signing of the trails.

Former Pinnacles Chief Ranger Ed Carlson and his wife, Cary, Park Ranger, contributed much information to us over several years.

Thanks also to Bill Lester, Chief Ranger at Pinnacles, for his helpful suggestions.

The maps were provided by Lucy Sargeant.

Any errors, however, are those of the authors alone.

INTRODUCTION

Pinnacles National Monument is a rugged land set apart.
Oddly shaped spires and crags tower above the visitor and chaparral-clad hills provide cover for the monument's varied wildlife. Cool caves and steep-walled canyons offer relief from the summer heat and many of the trails entice the hiker to see what is around the next bend.

To appreciate all that Pinnacles National Monument has to offer, it is necessary to hike one or more of its trails. Some beckon the visitor upward in a strenuous manner into an intimacy with the high peaks and their fascinating volcanic structure. The easier destination for others will be the always-popular Moses Spring/Bear Gulch Caves Trail, where adventures await and where alcoves of greenery appear unexpectedly around bends below soaring spires and sheer walls.

Whatever the interest of the visitor to Pinnacles might be, its birds and wildlife, its rugged chaparral-covered topography or the always incredible geological features, the trails will lead there for an hour or a day.

The monument, established on January 16, 1908 by President Theodore Roosevelt, now contains more than 16,000 acres. Over 80 percent consists of steep, chaparral-covered slopes that are readily accessible on scenic trails of varying length and steepness.

Pinnacles is primarily a hiker's area because of its relatively small size and the fragile nature and inaccessible locations of its principal ecological features. The major interests for visitors within the monument include the spectacular pinnacles of volcanic origin, the ever popular "caves," the diverse vegetation and the wildlife.

Once the home of the California condor, whose very survival is now threatened, the monument is still blessed with many species of birds, both migratory and permanent, as well as a variety of other wildlife.

The rough, rocky and arid landscape of the monument, which caps the low Gabilan mountain range, is about 125 miles southeast of

San Francisco, 75 miles southeast of San Jose and approximately 300 miles northwest of Los Angeles.

The highest point of the monument is North Chalone Peak at 3,304 feet, while the lowest point is just above 800 feet where Chalone Creek crosses the boundary on the southeasterly side.

The major visitor area on the eastern side of the monument is 34 miles south of Hollister and is reached from the north via State Highway 25. It can also be reached from King City via Highway G13 and State Highway 25. The four miles of Hwy. 146 lead from State 25 to the park boundary just beyond the privately operated Pinnacles Campground.

The entrance to the west side of the monument is a twelve-mile drive from Soledad on Highway 146, a good but steep, narrow and winding secondary road that is not recommended for trailers or motor homes. **It is not a through drive.** The Chaparral picnic area, a small campground and a ranger station are located here. Trails connect both sides of the monument and lead to the main areas of interest but no road joins the east and west sides.

Those wishing to see the pinnacles from near a road can best do so from the west side, where the jagged spires of the high peaks rise in a spectacular fashion.

HISTORY

Anthropologists believe that the Pinnacles area has been intermittently occupied by small groups of people. It is known that the Coastanoans eked out a marginal living in this rugged land.

The lack of water during the summer, however, suggests that the two local subgroups of the Coastanoans, the Chalon and the Matsun, probably visited from the Salinas River and other valleys that were more suited for year-round living. Acorns were their main food. Deer, rabbits and birds were hunted with bows and arrows or throwing sticks, and fish were caught in the meandering Salinas River.

The expansion of the Spanish mission system, along with widespread disease, all but eliminated the Coastanoans. By the time anthropologists began to study them, the culture was almost extinct.

The evidence of a large projectile point found at Pinnacles and subsequently dated at 2,000 years, indicates that the area was visited at a much earlier time, perhaps by ancestors of the Coastanoans.

One intriguing legend has it that high in the Gabilan Mountains are one or more lost Spanish silver mines. Their existence was kept in great secrecy by the padres from Mission San Carlos Borromeo (Carmel). Not long after the mission's establishment in 1770, large amounts of silver found its way into the religious ornaments of this and other missions. All mining stopped when the Americans arrived. Supposedly the mines were covered and a curse was put on anyone who ventured near, with death to strike anyone, Indian or Spaniard, who led an American to the mines.

Over the years many people have searched the Gabilan Range in vain trying to locate the lost mines. A story is told that in 1850, while in thick fog, a prospector stumbled upon a mine. He spent the night there, and the next morning headed for the nearest cattle camp with some ore samples. The cattle-camp crew spent five days searching for the mine, but never found it.

In 1874, Sheriff B.F. Ross of San Benito County, while in pursuit of horse thieves, found a smelter but could not locate a mine. It is believed the smelter dated from the days of the Spaniards.

An engineer for the California Division of Mines, Oliver Bowen, accidentally discovered a mine high in the Gabilan Range while making a survey for lime deposits in 1957. The mine fit the description of the legend which said that Soledad Mission could be seen from near the mine, which was hidden by pines and high in the mountains. This old silver mine is located about fifteen miles from Pinnacles.

Mining has occurred over the years within the boundaries of the monument. The Copper Mountain Mining Company once operated in the Old Pinnacles (westside) region. Another mine was located near the headquarters area. The mines have not been worked since they were included within the monument boundaries.

Another legend says that the notorious outlaw, Tiburcio Vasquez, may have used the Pinnacles region as a hideout from the law. He killed an American constable, William Harmount, when the lawman tried to arrest a companion of Vasquez after a disturbance at a Monterey dance hall.

Vasquez and his gang were feared throughout Central California as they continued to kill, pillage and plunder. Many times, they were pursued by the law only to disappear into the safety of the rugged crags.

At Snyder's Store in Tres Pinos (now Paicines), Vasquez and one of his men killed three people during a holdup. After the robbery, Vasquez reportedly stashed the loot in the caves at Pinnacles before fleeing to the Los Angeles area. The money has never been found. Most believe its presence is only a legend.

The bandit's luck finally ran out. A tip led to a sheriff's posse surprising the outlaw in a house west of Los Angeles. He was brought to trial, and his life of crime ended on March 19, 1875, when he was hanged in San Jose.

The valleys surrounding what is now Pinnacles Monument were settled beginning in 1850, when the land became available for homesteading. In the next decade or two, settlers began to use the area they called "Palisades" for recreation, social gatherings and picnics.

Then, in 1891, Schuyler Hain arrived from Michigan. He immediately was impressed with the rugged crags. He worked tirelessly for fifteen years toward preserving this unique area. Hain spoke to many groups, wrote articles and guided numerous people through his beloved Pinnacles. In large part, it was his efforts that led to this becoming a national monument.

It was Hain who enlisted the second ardent supporter of the Pinnacles preservation movement, Dr. David Starr Jordan, an early president of Stanford University. The unfaltering efforts of these two men, and many other supporters, resulted in President Theodore Roosevelt establishing Pinnacles National Monument in 1908.

The Pinnacles Lodge was built in 1925, and stood near the Visitor Center. The Lodge, known for its good food and reasonable rates, was popular with visitors for 23 years. The associated cabins were originally constructed to house the crews that built the road up to Bear Gulch.

Lodge operations stopped in 1948 and the old wooden building fell into disrepair. Sadly, in 1955 the old lodge was dismantled. Park employees now work in the cabins that once housed lodge guests.

Created in 1933 and active for nearly ten years, the Civilian Conservation Corp has left an unforgettable legacy of park and recreation facilities throughout the nation. Although generally inexperienced at first, the young people were quickly molded into a first-class work force under the direction and guidance of permanent government personnel, including members of the National Park Service and the U.S. Forest Service.

Their work could not be financially duplicated today. Projects in Pinnacles National Monument that are still in use stand as a tribute

The reservoir, a lovely little body of water above the Moses Spring/Bear Gulch Caves Trail. A dam constructed by the C.C.C. impounded the water of Bear Creek.

to this great era of park advancement.

A stone dam created the Bear Gulch Reservoir which once furnished water for park headquarters and is now a lovely small lake for visitors to enjoy. On the way to the reservoir, the trail passes through the tunnel carved in rock on the Moses Spring Trail. A stairway and handrails safeguard the passage of hikers along steep rock faces near the top on the High Peaks Trail.

Some of the bridge, tunnel and stone projects, however, were completed prior to the advent of the C.C.C. The High Peaks Trail was built during the tenure of W.I. Hawkins, the second custodian of the monument. Hawkins Peak, the highest point in the High Peaks, was named in his honor.

Visitors hiking the Tunnel Trail near High Peaks will marvel at the 100 feet excavated through the volcanic rock. The high concrete bridge adjacent to the tunnel is virtually irreplaceable.

Hikers using the Balconies Trail should note the large hand-hewn blocks of rhyolite that support the trail on steep hillsides.

Historically, many of the facilities still in use today, trails, bridges, tunnels and buildings, have endured for 60 years or more. They stand as a tribute to farsighted park planners of the early years of the monument's development.

The entrance to the Balconies Caves from the east. Some stonework done years ago has levelled the entrance.

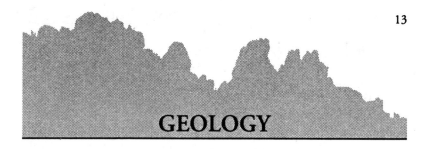

GEOLOGY

The geology of the Pinnacles National Monument is complex, but certain obvious features of this rugged topography are of interest to even the most casual observer:

— The dramatic rocky spires of the high peaks and the reservoir area, plus the equally awesome sheer rock faces of Machete Ridge and the Balconies. What are they and how did they reach their present form?

— The ever-popular "caves" of Bear Gulch and the Balconies, which offer such a pleasant and cool respite from the summer heat. They also prove to be an exciting adventure for visitors of all ages. How were they formed?

— The Chalone Creek streambed, which contains fascinating rocks of many types including granite, although the towering spires of Pinnacles National Monument are not composed of this rock. Where did the granite come from?

Geologically, the formation is known as the Pinnacles Volcanics and its rocks have been dated by potassium-argon methods to 23½ million years of age (early Miocene time). All rocks, whether they are volcanic, sedimentary or metamorphic, are composed of minerals, one or two or many. Volcanic rocks derive their appearance, structure and texture from their origin as molten material deep within the earth. Basically, if this material, called magma, cooled slowly under the surface of the earth, the individual minerals have more time to crystallize and grow into larger form, and coarse-textured rock like granite can occur. If the magma poured out of fissures onto the surface of the earth or emerged as a gas-choked explosive material from the vent of a volcano, it cooled rapidly. The individual minerals did not have time to grow to maturity, so a finer-textured rock is the result.

Some of the rocks of Pinnacles have been altered by thermal (heat), chemical or climatic activity (such as in the caves). Most, however, originated as limited lava flows from fissures on the surface and cooled rapidly. Thus they are much finer in texture than granite. These rocks are called rhyolite. Many studies have shown that over 90 percent of the Pinnacles Volcanics consists of three rock types: *rhyolitic breccia, massive rhyolite* and *flow-banded rhyolite*. The breccia is composed of small irregular fragments of rhyolite that became imbedded in still-molten flows of the same material before cooling took place. Massive rhyolite presents itself as an homogenous mass. The flow-banded rhyolite takes on a layered appearance resembling the strata of some sedimentary rocks. A flow would emerge, cool and perhaps have some surface erosion before being covered by another, possibly slightly different appearing flow. This presents a banded appearance at a distance throughout much of the pinnacled portion of the monument. These bands and flow structures dip generally westward in a structure called a *homocline*.

The inherent mineral composition gives rocks their color. The volcanic rocks of Pinnacles are high in minerals of the feldspar and quartz variety and low in iron and are relatively light in color like most granite. Others, such as lava flows of basalt, are lower in the feldspars and quartz and high in darker-colored minerals such as iron, and are, therefore, quite dark in color. Several excellent identification charts of rocks based on color, texture, weight, mineral composition

The view just before the entrance to the Bear Gulch Caves. Note the differential erosion by wind and water, which has created huge blocks of rhyolite.

and other factors are available, as are useful books on the subject.

One might ask, if granite was formed slowly under the surface of the earth, why is it now exposed throughout the high Sierra Nevada and, in places, near the seashore? In the process of uplift and mountain building over millions of years, the agents of erosion, running water including ocean activity, wind and glacial ice, have stripped the original overlying cover from the underlying granite, exposing it to view.

To the west, the Pinnacles Volcanics rest unconformably on older eroded bedrock granite. The water of Chalone Creek has had upstream erosional access to some of this granite beyond the northwest part of the monument, so many small granite rocks are found in the bed of the creek, which, in part, marks the trace of the ancient Chalone Creek fault.

A hiker near the entrance to the Moses Springs Caves. A flashlight is needed for the journey through the dark cavern. This is an adventure for people of all ages. The caves, however, should not be entered in periods of flooding.

Over many millions of years following the cessation of volcanic activity, some of which was of an explosive nature, uplift occurred. Running water physically and chemically eroded several deep, narrow canyons within the Pinnacles Volcanics. More erosion by water in flow joints, assisted by wind erosion, formed huge boulders above the canyons, which eventually were loosened by gravity and possibly by earth movement. These boulders and large fragments slid into the narrow canyons but were too large to fill the gorges. So, in places they formed a roof over the canyons, resulting in the "caves" of Bear Gulch and the Balconies. Running water over the ages has further enlarged the caves that the visitor sees and enjoys today.

The continents are parts of what are called *tectonic plates*, which are large segmented blocks of the earth's crust. They shift, break and often separate, causing earthquakes and faulting.

Millions of years ago, two of these huge plates began drifting apart. The western one, the Pacific, has been moving northward at an average rate of about one and one-half inches a year during that time. The awesome 600-mile long San Andreas fault, which with some of its adjacent faults is responsible for many of the devastating earthquakes of the region, is believed to mark the contact between the Pacific and the North American plates in this area.

The pinnacles as the visitor sees them today were not born here. This spectacular scenic mass began 195 miles south, where the Pinnacles Volcanics were part of a rock unit now called the Neenach Volcanics (located along State Highway 138 between Lancaster and Gorman). The San Andreas fault separated the two parts and, perhaps 20 million years ago, the western half began its northward movement (called strike-slip displacement). This movement is still taking place, but since the establishment in 1908 of the Pinnacles National Monument, only a small amount of movement has taken place. At this rate it will be millions of years before the monument will have moved northward to take its place alongside San Francisco!

An even more disturbing suggestion is that millions of years hence, Los Angeles will have migrated north and will occupy the present site of Pinnacles National Monument. Following these grim prospects, it has been suggested that the San Andreas fault be bolted together to prevent more northerly movement!

In a more serious vein, many will note that the present-day San Andreas fault is actually located about four miles to the east of the monument's eastern boundary (in the valley of the San Benito River).

The major traceable break in the monument is the Chalone Creek fault, which is partly responsible for the stream-eroded valley of Chalone Creek. This fault has been traced both north and south of Pinnacles for a total distance of about 52 miles. Many miles to the south, it joins the San Andreas fault. Evidence now points to the fact that during the last few miles of the northward movement of the Pinnacles Volcanics, the Chalone Creek fault was actually the ancient trace of the San Andreas. Subsequent earth movement over the past few million years has separated the two faults. The Pinnacles fault zone, where the westward-dipping rhyolitic rocks come in contact with the older granitic rocks of the Gabilan Range, is roughly along a north-south line just to the west of the Chaparral Picnic Area. This is difficult to see, however, because of dense chaparral growth.

The rocks that the hikers will see the most frequently, then, are the rhyolitic-breccias of the high peaks. These are primarily flows in which are imbedded angular fragments of more rhyolite. The rock faces composed of this material are frequented by climbers. This is also the predominant material of the spectacular Machete Ridge and the vertical walls of the Balconies.

A large area to the east of North Chalone Peak consists of massive fine-textured gray to pink rhyolite, but it is largely concealed by chaparral. On the west edge of the monument, banded rhyolite flows uncomformably overlie the older granite.

Small amounts of other rock types are present, including andesite and dacite, tuff (a cemented volcanic ash), and pumice, but the rhyolitic breccia flows and massive rhyolitic rocks predominate.

This is only a brief summary of the geologic story that has spanned 23½ million years. Another few million years may see the pinnacles reduced to a flat plain by erosion. Perhaps, however, more molten material will find its way up from deep within the earth and, amid explosive activity, flow over the surface. Still later, deep erosion by running water and wind may sculpture a newer and even grander mass of pinnacles. And, who knows, someday they, too, may find their way via the San Andreas fault another 100 miles north to the San Francisco Bay area!

NATURAL HISTORY

"Natural history" refers to the great diversity of plants and animals and the study of their characteristics, encompassing their distribution, behavior, life cycles and ecological relationships. Included are the smallest of living things, from insects to the lichens on the rocks, organisms that most visitors may not even notice.

The authors intend to briefly describe only the more obvious features of the monument. For those wishing more comprehensive information, please check the references. Some fine publications are available in the Bear Gulch Visitor Center. Most will refer to scientific as well as common names.

Scientific names (usually Latin) are used to identify a plant or animal specifically because many have various common names that may be confusing. For example, there are many pines in the world, all with a generic name of Pinus. However, there is only one *Pinus sabiniana*, a native of the western United States now generally called gray or bull pine. There are two manzanitas in Pinnacles: The Mexican, *Arctostaphylos pungens*, and the big-berried, *Arctostaphylos glauca*.

Biotic Communities

Most biologists recognize four major and reasonably well-defined biological communities in the monument. Each in general has its own assemblage of plants and animals, although some, like the gray pine, grow freely in all four. These communities are: the *riparian*, the *rock-scree*, the *chaparral* and the *woodland-savannah*.

Riparian Community

The riparian, the stream valleys, will be explored first. In areal extent, it is not a large zone, encompassing only three percent of the monument. It is characterized by an assemblage of plants and animals that need a fairly abundant supply of water throughout the year. The valleys of Chalone Creek, Bear Gulch and West Chalone Creek are the most visited of this water-requiring community. In the heart of the summer, even Chalone Creek is seemingly dry, with only an occasional standing pool to reflect the overhead beauty. But don't be misled; the water is there just under the surface and the plants that require it exist here. Usually, sufficient surface water remains to give the animals enough to drink. During the remainder of the year, all the intermittent streams carry considerable amounts of water. Chalone Creek can become a small river at times.

Trees, the most obvious plants, help shade and control the growth of many smaller plants beneath. The gray pine, although extremely drought resistant and found throughout the monument, is prominent in the stream valleys and elsewhere, with its peculiar crooked growth habit. It has three long needles in each sheath and the short, thick, heavy cones lying beneath the trees are very characteristic. It is the only pine here.

Other obvious trees of the community are the huge, spreading, deciduous valley oaks (*Quercus lobata*), the largest tree of the oak family. The also large but evergreen coast live-oak (*Quercus agrifolia*) is also common. In the fall, its green foliage stands out against the surroundings of brown, parched-appearing vegetation. The large, white-barked

Leaving the Chaparral visitor area on the Balconies Trail through a pleasant grassy meadow under the shade of large valley and live oaks.

California sycamore (*Plantanus racemosa*) is conspicuous, as is the Fremont cottonwood (*Populus fremontii*). Two small willows, the sandbar and the arroyo, (*Salix spp.*), are common along stream courses.

Early spring will witness the green streamsides alive with color. Roses, gooseberries, chainferns, blackberries and hedgenettles are prominent. Be alert for that infamous character, the three-leaved poison oak (*Toxicodendron diversiloba*). It can be prostrate, shrub-like, or climb as a vine many feet up into a tree.

Birdlife is rich and varied. Two essentials, food and shelter, are here in abundance. The visitors interested in birds look eagerly for glimpses of the white-breasted nuthatch, the black-headed grosbeak, woodpeckers, hummingbirds, jays and many others. Hawks, turkey vultures and an occasional golden eagle are often seen soaring over the ridges and stream valleys.

Mammals are usually more obvious and are of great interest to young and old. The nocturnal raccoon, although fun to watch, can be the scourge of a campground. Coons have been known to enter tents in search of chow. Secure all food at night.

Deer can be seen in the middle of the day, but are more commonly observed during the feeding times of early morning and late evening. Ground squirrels and chipmunks frequent the picnic areas. More elusive, but often spotted, are foxes and coyotes. Occasionally, those most furtive of cats, the bobcat and mountain lion, are reported, but usually in the more remote areas.

Many reptiles are here, including salamanders, lizards and snakes. Only one, the Northern Pacific rattlesnake, can be harmful to man. In April and May and again in early fall, be watchful when on or off the trails. They coil when danger approaches but only strike when they feel radically disturbed. If you see one, let it be!

Chaparral Community

Approximately 82 percent of Pinnacles National Monument consists of the distinctive plant community called *chaparral*. Apparently the name is derived from the Spanish *chaparro* or scrub oak.

Within only a few feet of rise from the lower stream valleys, the brushy chaparral will commence. Many plants are found here, but the greater portion of the vegetation consists of three hardy shrubs, the red-barked manzanita (*Arctostaphylos sp.*), the buckbrush or ceanothus (*Ceanothus cuneatus*), and chamise or greasewood (*Adenostoma fasciculatum*). Off-the-trail travel can verge on the impossible because of the thick, spiny and virtually impenetrable cover presented by these three species. In another section, the authors have outlined the effect of fire, intentional or accidental, on the vegetation of the chaparral.

The scarcity of water, especially during the summer months, is reflected in the ability, through adaptation, of the plants and many of the animals to survive and grow here. The only tree of any size in the chaparral is the gray pine, whose roots can penetrate many feet into the soil and cracks in the rocks in its quest for water. The holly-leaf cherry (*Prunus ilicifolia*) with its creamy-white spring flowers grows here as does the California toyon or Christmas berry (*Heteromeles arbutifolia*). The seeds and the berries were used by the Native Americans of the area for various purposes.

The most characteristic bird of the chaparral is the wrentit, whose distinctive call is commonly heard. Other smaller birds often seen are the California thrasher and the brown towhee. A flash of grayish-blue will mark the presence of the scrub jay. Two small raptors of the community, the sharp-shinned hawk and the sparrow hawk, are here.

Snakes are not often seen, but if a rattlesnake is to be spotted, it most often will be in the chaparral. The enemy of the rattlesnake, the king snake, is also here.

Bobcats prefer the seclusion of the chaparral and the rocks above. They are normally nocturnal hunters, but are occasionally seen in the daytime. Deer are quite common from the stream valleys to the base of the high rocks. Rabbits abound, but are more often seen in the open areas of the riparian and the woodland-savannah.

The ecological importance of the chaparral to the surrounding communities is a vital one.

Rock-Scree Community

The term *rock-scree* is fitting for this rocky region. Lack of water, rapid drying conditions in the hot summer temperatures and a generally poor, thin soil are the most important factors in this community, which encompasses a scant three percent of the monument. Often, only a few feet separate the chaparral from the rock-scree.

Generally speaking, very few plants of any size exist here except occasionally where an eroded hollow has accumulated some soil. The most obvious plants to be noticed by observing visitors are the lichens, which grow on the rocks in profusion. These tiny moss-like plants, actually a fungus-algae partnership, cover the rocks to such an extent that they lend color. Light greens, browns, faint reds and pale orange are common. Another form of lichen can be seen hanging from oak branches.

This community does support a population of small animals, with an ecological interaction between them and the plants continuously taking place. Birds nest here. The turkey vulture, a scavenger, and the golden eagle are the largest birds seen in the monument.

Two or three nesting pairs of peregrine falcons used to be seen high on the rocks of the Balconies. Peregrines have been called the fastest of all American flying birds, and reportedly have been clocked in dives up to 175 miles per hour. There are hopes that a recent cross-fostering program will bring them back. There are, however, nesting prairie falcons. These close relatives of the peregrine are also fast birds (in fact they may fly faster than peregrines).

The Park Service is actively researching and protecting the prairie falcons and golden eagles. The California condor, long gone from the monument, used to nest among its high spires.

Bobcats are here and the elusive mountain lion is still occasionally spotted. More often seen and heard among the high peaks, however, are the not-so-elusive rock climbers (*Homo sapiens*). They are reported to be increasing in population.

Woodland-Savannah Community

The distinctive zone called the *woodland-savannah* consists of grasslands dotted with trees. Its relief is usually gentle and at Pinnacles most commonly occurs on the north and east-facing slopes and in the wider stream valleys. As usual, water, soil and temperature are limiting factors for both plants and animals. The only two large trees in the sloped areas are the gray pine and the blue oak (*Quercus douglasii*), and the use of the word large is only relative. Both are extremely drought-resistant and send long roots deep into the soil and rocks in search of water. The wider valleys are dominated by valley oaks and coast live oaks. Many species of grasses are found in the open areas of the woodland-savannah community. However, most of the original native bunch grasses have been replaced by exotic European species.

The California quail is a distinctive bird of the grassland although seen in other communities as well. Its principal enemies, the gray fox, red-tailed hawk and bobcat, are found here, also. The commonly-seen mule or black-tailed deer are often a pleasant sight in the open grasslands. Rabbits, too, abound here. It has been estimated that this community only embraces about twelve percent of the monument, but its ecological importance is far greater than its areal extent.

The visitor who is interested in knowing about this complex ecological life will find much information in the visitor center. Regularly scheduled interpretive programs presented by the Park Service naturalists are well worth attending.

PRESCRIBED BURNING

Traditionally in our forests, grasslands and outdoor recreation areas, fire has been looked upon as a dreaded enemy instead of a natural phenomenon. Over the years, great sums of money, both public and private, have been spent on projects related to the prevention, detection and ultimate suppression of wildfires. Governmental agencies, notably the U.S. Forest Service, National Park Service and state forestry organizations, have mounted impressive anti-wildfire programs. The nationwide Smokey Bear campaign has probably been the most successful.

"Drown your campfire, every spark," and, "Only you can prevent forest fires," have become familiar slogans to all frequent outdoor recreation visitors. The time-honored forest lookout system, summertime standby fire crews and trained smokejumpers have all played a part in the attempt to control fires.

Lightning storms have actually set more disastrous forest fires than have people, but even Smokey Bear is helpless to prevent these.

Often visitors hiking the Pinnacles Monument trails, particularly through the chaparral, will see where large sections have recently burned. They see the blackened area and smell the pungent result. Most probably assume lightning or careless smokers are to blame. When they learn that many of these fires have been set intentionally, some are indignant. Why, they ask?

The philosophy and practice of controlled or prescribed burning as an ally on certain forest and grassland areas is now recognized and accepted as an important tool in forest management. Following is a summary of the **why** of prescribed burning.

Overprotect a certain forest area for fifty years and the result will be a tremendous overabundance of understory vegetation and organic cover on the forest floor. When tinder-dry in the summer and susceptible to lightning strikes or man's carelessness, a disastrous conflagration can result.

Fire ecologists contend that the best control is to intentionally use fire as a tool to prevent this potentially dangerous buildup of fire-susceptible material as it was in nature before man intervened. This makes sense. Some loss of esthetics and wildlife habitat may result, it is true, but not the tragedy that can follow an uncontrollable wind-driven wildfire. The classic example was the Peshtigo, Wisconsin, fire of 1879, which claimed 1,500 lives and scarred thousands of acres.

Following an adequate surface fire, growth will begin the first year and accelerate until maturity. Dr. Robert Sweeney, Professor Emeritus from San Francisco State University and a noted fire ecologist, has stated, "Such vegetations that are dependent on fire and that are frequently burned, reproduce in abundance and prosper." He further states that some needed plants only sprout following fire and that seeds of these have lain dormant for as long as 60 years where fires have been suppressed.

Because of a long history of fire suppression, almost twenty percent of the chaparral of Pinnacles is overmature and dying. Little new growth is evident in such areas, and the chaparral's value as food and shelter for wildlife is greatly lessened. Studies show that manzanita and ceanothus (buckbrush) seeds germinate well after the heat of surface fires has occurred, and chamise root burls sprout vigorously.

Prescribed fires serve two general purposes at Pinnacles. One is to develop a wide buffer zone, often called a "fire line." This strategy is designed to help fire crews have a reasonable chance to control fires approaching the park from outside lands, as well as to keep desirable fires within the park.

Secondly, prescribed and controlled fires are used to replace the results of naturally-occurring fires on as near a real-time basis as possible. Fire may also be used as a tool to control the invasion of chaparral vegetation into the woodland community. Species such as the gray pine will be forced back to their rightful ecological balance and the development of biological species will resume as it should in a natural area.

Some fire scarring will briefly result, but new growth soon eliminates this. The controlled use of fire will result in a great overall benefit to the natural areas affected.

It is not meant to be implied that fire suppression should be eliminated on all our forests and grasslands but only in areas where the prescribed use of fires may be beneficial. The chaparral vegetation of Pinnacles National Monument is one of these areas where the prescribed use of fires may be beneficial. The chaparral vegetation of Pinnacles National Monument is one of these areas.

CAMPING

There are 18 small walk-in tent campsites in the Chaparral visitor area, but they are not suitable for large family use. This is a campground that primarily serves hikers and climbers.

The privately operated Pinnacles Campground is located just outside the eastern boundary of the monument, off Highway 146. There are 78 individual sites with adequate space for privacy between them. In addition, there are 14 large group sites at considerable distance from the individual or family areas. Electrical hookups are available. Water and restrooms are conveniently located.

A store with limited supplies, a pool and showers are located at the entrance of the campground. The large unheated pool is a welcome facility at the close of a warm day of hiking and sightseeing.

Both campgrounds are first come/first served. Group campground sites at Pinnacles Campground may be reserved by calling (408)389-4462.

THE CLIMATE

The monument, although only 35 miles from the Pacific Ocean, is located in a semi-arid climatic area. The dominant coast ranges across the Salinas River Valley to the west restrict most of the marine influence and hot, dry summers with cool winters are the result. Temperatures of over 100^0 are not uncommon from May through September, while the cool winter season from November to April brings about 16 inches of rain. Daytime temperature variations between early morning and afternoon can exceed 50^0. Snow occasionally falls on the higher elevations.

Consistently, the most pleasant weather and the heaviest visitation to the monument occur in the spring and the fall, especially during the months of March and April and again in October and November. At any time during the winter months, however, pleasant days do occur, and hikers can enjoy an outing while meeting fewer people on the trails.

ROCK CLIMBING

Hikers in the rocky and pinnacled areas of the monument will often hear voices echoing among the rocks. With careful observation, one can usually discern people clinging to a wall of rock or perched on a ledge high above the trail while seemingly entwined in a maze of ropes and slings of colorful hues.

These people are engaging in one of the monument's most popular and certainly the most spectacular activity, technical rock climbing. There are hundreds of charted routes of varying difficulty, ranging from "bouldering" of twenty vertical feet to high spectacular face climbs of several hundred feet. The latter are only for the expert rock climbers.

Nothing daunts the climbing rangers more than to observe a car full of obviously inexperienced people arrive outfitted with their "clothesline" ropes and determined to find out what this madness of rock climbing is all about.

In the Pinnacles National Monument and elsewhere, technical rock climbing (one rather specialized phase of mountaineering), can be an exhilarating adventure, but only for those who have the basic qualifications. Rock climbing techniques are taught by many outdoor clubs and schools. The most important ingredient of any climbing group is a knowledgeable and patient leader who inspires confidence, but who will keep the climb within the degree of skills and abilities of his party members.

Where any outdoor activity becomes popular, in time someone will write a guide. Rock climbing in the Pinnacles is no exception. A popular book that is widely used today, Dave Rubine's *Climber's Guide - Pinnacles National Monument*, was preceded by several others as well as Sierra Club papers from the early 1950's.

Almost every conceivable rock climb in the monument is now charted and a standard classification for each climb is used. These range from Class 1, which is only off-the-trail hiking, to the Class 5 group which contains the extremely difficult climbs for experts only.

However, climbing at Pinnacles is a managed activity. Access trails

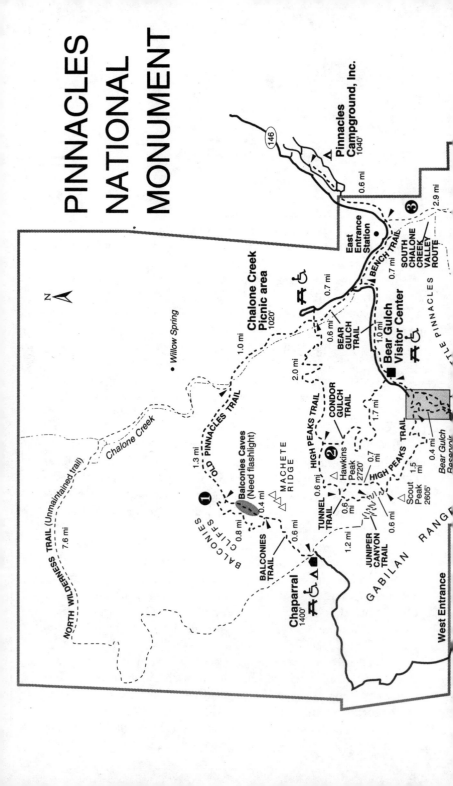

PINNACLES NATIONAL MONUMENT

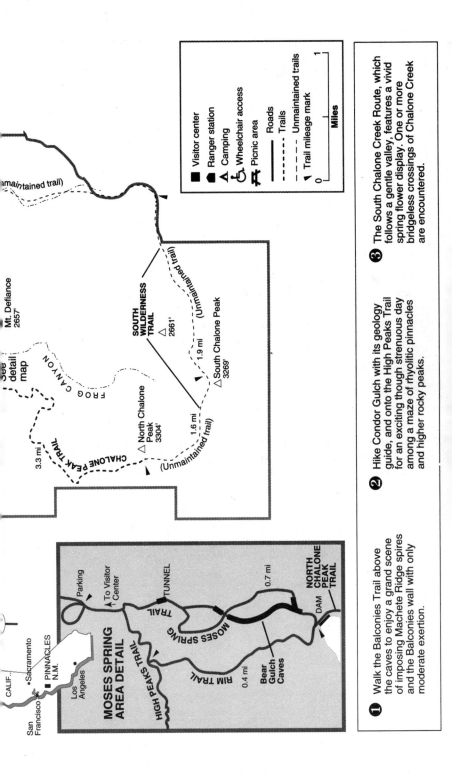

MOSES SPRING AREA DETAIL

San Francisco · Sacramento
PINNACLES N.M.
Los Angeles
CALIF.

To Visitor Center

Parking

TUNNEL

MOSES SPRING TRAIL

HIGH PEAKS TRAIL

RIM TRAIL

Bear Gulch Caves

0.7 mi

0.4 mi

NORTH CHALONE PEAK TRAIL

DAM

Mt. Defiance 2657'

See detail map

FROG CANYON

CHALONE PEAK TRAIL

3.3 mi

North Chalone Peak 3304'

SOUTH WILDERNESS TRAIL

2661'

1.6 mi

(Unmaintained trail)

South Chalone Peak 3269'

1.9 mi

(Unmaintained trail)

(Unmaintained trail)

- Visitor center
- Ranger station
- Camping
- Wheelchair access
- Picnic area
  Roads
  Trails
  Unmaintained trails
- Trail mileage mark

0 — Miles — 1

1 Walk the Balconies Trail above the caves to enjoy a grand scene of imposing Machete Ridge spires and the Balconies wall with only moderate exertion.

2 Hike Condor Gulch with its geology guide, and onto the High Peaks Trail for an exciting though strenuous day among a maze of rhyolitic pinnacles and higher rocky peaks.

3 The South Chalone Creek Route, which follows a gentle valley, features a vivid spring flower display. One or more bridgeless crossings of Chalone Creek are encountered.

to several climbing areas have been improved or rerouted to control erosion. Green plastic netting is used, along with signs, to effectively close over-used access routes to the rocks, and to attempt to control "short-cutting" of the trails. In addition, a number of popular climbing areas and rock formations are closed annually during prairie falcon and golden eagle nesting season (January to June/July).

No new routes may be established.

It is suggested that all climbers check information boards located near the Moses Spring Trailhead in the East District or the Chaparral parking lot in the West District (or the ranger station in either district) for up-to-date information.

The majority of climbs in the monument are found in one of three areas: The Reservoir, the High Peaks and the Chaparral (west) side, where the Balconies and Machete Ridge climbs are the most accessible. Every climb is descriptively named and these range from the Toilet Seat to Spasm Block. Climbers near the reservoir and above the Moses Spring and Bear Gulch Caves are probably the most observable to the interested visitor.

The rock of the monument is not considered good rock for climbing as is the tough, glaciated granite of the Yosemite Valley, for example. It is mostly volcanic breccia (see Geology section) that consists of angular fragments of rock imbedded in a matrix of hardened ash and other volcanic material. As a result, the hand and footholds for the climber consist of protruding nubbins, which are sometimes not too solid and often rounded. Because of the jointing of the rock, the ledges are often down-sloping. For climbing security, specialty rock devices are almost an essential on difficult climbs on the relatively unstable volcanic rocks of the Pinnacles. However, no power drills are permitted.

THE TRAIL SYSTEM

The trail system is the backbone of Pinnacles National Monument. If the visitor is coming to view spectacular scenery from a parking lot, he can do much better by driving to Yosemite. It is not to be implied that everyone visiting Pinnacles should be prepared to engage in the ordeal of a long, steep trail hike, although several of the hikes can be arduous.

The monument, however, contains shorter and more pleasant hikes that still take the visitor into the quiet intimacy of a wilderness-like experience. These range from the lovely April flower fields along the South Chalone Creek Valley Route south of the campground to the spectacular spires and walls of Machete Ridge and the Balconies via the Balconies or Old Pinnacles Trails at any season of the year.

Regardless of which trail you choose, go prepared with sturdy hiking shoes or boots, adequate and comfortable loose clothing plus a sun-shade hat. If you plan a lengthy trek, take a water bottle and a lunch. If not in shape, set a slow but steady and rhythmic pace; it is always surprising how far one can go without any undue discomfort other than a bit of sweating. ALLOW PLENTY OF TIME FOR THE RETURN TRIP! Use common sense, enjoy, but don't overdo.

Some of the trails can be hiked as loops, but to complete most loops can lead to an arduous day. Car pickups between the east and west centers should not be attempted as no roads cut through the monument and those around it are very long. Therefore, hikers on a day jaunt should return to their starting point unless they have planned another alternative carefully. Check distances and elevation gains. Conservatively calculate your speed at one and one-half to two miles per hour. The authors recognize that most of the trails can be hiked in either direction. However, for the sake of brevity, the description of a trail will be in the direction most hikers take. But where possible, the trail features will be described in a manner that we hope can be recognized in reverse.

The trail descriptions are divided into three sections corresponding to the location of the trailhead. At the beginning of each trail description are three points of information: trail difficulty, the distance in miles and kilometers and the relief.

Follow the National Park Service safety precautions. Stay on the trails and respect the attempt to control "short-cutting" by the use of signs and green netting. Leave the rock climbing to the experienced. Follow the simple rules. Hike to your heart's content. Observe carefully and enjoy the many vistas and the natural history of Pinnacles National Monument. That, we like to believe, is what you came for.

THE TRAILS

SECTION I – Hikes beginning at or close to the **Pinnacles Campground** (1,040 ft., 317 mts.) or at the **Chalone Creek Trailhead** (1,020 ft., 311 mts.) on the east side of the monument.

    A. **Bench Trail** from the Pinnacles Campground near group site #79, to the junction with the Bear Gulch Trail leading left to the visitor center or right to the Chalone Creek Trailhead.

    B. **Old Pinnacles Trail** to its junction with the Balconies Trail, which leads to the Chaparral visitor area via the Balconies Caves or above them on the Balconies Cliff Trail.

    C. **Bear Gulch Trail** to the visitor center from the Chalone Creek Trailhead.

    D. **High Peaks Trail** to several possible destinations.

    E. **North Wilderness Trail** to Chaparral.

    F. **South Chalone Creek Valley Route** (unmaintained) along eastern boundary as a pleasant stroll along Chalone Creek from the highway or as a connection with the South Wilderness Trail (Section II-F).

SECTION II – Hikes beginning at or close to the Bear Gulch Visitor Center and Park Headquarters (1,280 ft., 390 mts.) on the east side of the monument.

    A. **Moses Spring/Bear Gulch Caves Trail** to the caves and the reservoir.

    B. **Rim Trail** from the reservoir to junction of the High Peaks Trail. An alternate scenic short hike either before or after the Bear Gulch Caves.

    C. **High Peaks Trail** with several destinations. (See Section I-D).

    D. **Condor Gulch Trail** with several possible loops and destinations.

    E. **Chalone Peak Trail** to North Chalone Peak.

    F. **South Chalone Peak and South Wilderness Trail.** Connects

North Chalone Peak with the South Chalone Creek Valley Route. (See Section I-F). Note cautions in text.

SECTION III – Hikes beginning at the Chaparral Trailhead (1,400 ft., 427 mts.) on the west side of the monument at the terminus of Highway 146 from Soledad.

    A. **Balconies Cliff and Balconies Caves Trails** to junction with Old Pinnacles (Section I-B).

    B. **Juniper Canyon Trail** to the high peaks area.

    C. **Tunnel Trail**, a short but steep section which is an alternate to the upper portion of the High Peaks Trail.

    D. **North Wilderness Trail** (See Section I-E).

SECTION I – PINNACLES CAMPGROUND OR CHALONE CREEK TRAILHEAD

A. **Bench Trail**
Degree of Difficulty: Easy
Distance: 1.2 miles (1.9 km) from Pinnacles Campground to junction with the Bear Gulch Trail.
Relief: Not over 59 feet.

For those who desire to leave their vehicles in the campground, the Bench Trail is one of convenience to reach other trailheads. It leaves the campground near Site #79 and extends southwest, where it enters the monument in a few minutes.

The trail climbs slightly beneath valley and coast live oaks and an occasional gray pine. It drops to Chalone Creek, where at 0.6 mile it passes the junction with the Chalone Creek Valley Route. Here it turns northwest and follows the creek to a footbridge and its junction with Bear Gulch Trail. If your destination is the signed trailhead adjacent to Chalone Creek Picnic Area, continue about another one-half mile on the Bear Gulch Trail along the west bank of Chalone Creek. If going to the visitor center, turn west on the moderate, scenic and shaded Bear Gulch Trail.

B. **Old Pinnacles Trail**
Difficulty: Easy, but scenic. Highly recommended for people with small children or for poorly-conditioned hikers.
Distance: 2.3 miles (3.7 km) to the junction with the Balconies Cliff Trail, which ascends to the right. The shaded Balconies Caves Trail to the left will reach and pass through the caves in only 0.4 mile. Another 0.6 mile will lead to Chaparral.

Relief: 220 feet to junction with Balconies Trails, 420 feet if the hike continues through the caves.

Physically, this is the least demanding longer trail hike in the park, but it leads to the base of some of the most spectacular rocky spires. Here are intimate views of the pinnacles and walls of Machete Ridge and the Balconies. It can be a rewarding hike for those interested in birds. Prairie falcons and golden eagles have been observed nesting high on the sheer rock walls of the Balconies.

The hike begins across the footbridge from the Chalone Creek Picnic area at the signed junction (which, however, gives destinations instead of trail names). The trail follows the creek as it climbs gently through open areas and beneath an occasional gray pine, with willows, live oaks and other stream-valley vegetation in evidence. In less than 0.5 mile, the trail crosses the creek on another footbridge. At about 1.0 mile, the main valley of Chalone Creek leads away to the north. This is the route of the scenic North Wilderness Trail described in Section I-E. The main valley is, in part, the trace of the ancient Chalone Creek fault. The rocky rubble in the creek bed includes granite, which underlies the rhyolitic volcanic rocks of the monument.

During the long summer season, both branches of the creek will be dry appearing, with only occasional pretty pools of water to reflect the overhead scenery.

Beyond the main valley junction, the first of several bridgeless creek crossings of the West Fork of Chalone Creek will be encountered. During much of the year, only small amounts of water will be in the channels, but during the rainy season, hikers may get their feet wet while fording the creek. As the gentle climb continues, several coast live oaks reach over the trail and on the left, a California juniper appears. Blue elderberries and California buckeyes are to be seen, and large gray pines lean over the trail. During the spring, the wildflower display is lovely both near the creek and on the adjacent hillsides.

In a short distance, the junction with the Balconies Cliff Trail is reached. It switchbacks up over the rocks at the base of the spectacular walls of the Balconies and finally descends toward Chaparral Picnic Area. The trail ahead, the Balconies Caves Trail, leads through a shaded, rocky canyon to the caves. This is a cool and delightful haven on a hot summer day. Above the caves entrance tower the lofty 400 foot spires of Machete Ridge.

The caves will probably prove to be the main objective of most parties, and after the trip through them to the major junction beyond (another 0.4 mile),the return can be made back through the caves or "over the top" (0.8 miles) on the Balconies Cliff Trail. This is the recommended return because of the rewarding views of the imposing rocks of Machete Ridge and the Balconies, which are sometimes termed, "Little Yosemite." Rock climbers are often heard and occasionally seen in this jumbled area.

C. **Bear Gulch Trail**

Difficulty: Moderate. The large variety of plant life is the keynote of this worthwhile hike. Can be hiked either way, with car pickup as convenient.

Distance: 1.7 miles (2.7 km) to Bear Gulch Visitor Center from start of trail across creek from the Chalone Creek Picnic Area.

Relief: 250 feet. A well-graded trail, mostly in the shade. Recommended for a warm day.

The trail undulates along the southwest bank of the creek for 0.5 mile, through vegetation that is partly stream valley and partly chaparral. The walk leads near or under willows, cottonwoods and coast live oaks. Ahead, the steep chaparral-covered hills and ridges rise

The imposing spires of Machete Ridge from above the Old Pinnacles and Balconies Trail junction.

abruptly above and beyond Chalone Creek, and a lone gray pine is silhouetted above a skyline ridge. Not a beautiful expanse of country by most standards, it is spiny, rough and inhospitable to hikers, with little or no water. The ridges are traversed at best by narrow and steep trails of deer and feral pigs. Viewed, however, with the shadows of early morning or late evening, this rugged chaparral country can exude an aura and personality all its own and not always unpleasant.

At the junction with the Bench Trail from Pinnacles Campground, turn west and follow Bear Gulch Creek as it climbs into the pretty and mostly shaded little valley of Bear Gulch. Two water-requiring trees are here, sycamores and willows. The gray-green foliage of the gray pine is seen on the steep slopes just above the trail.

The trail crosses the small tumbling creek several times on attractive footbridges. Watch for the display of ferns, with the goldback, delicate maidenhair and large fronds of the chain fern growing in damp, shaded habitats along the creek bed. Even in the summer when the stream is seemingly dry, water is not far under the surface.

In less than 1.0 mile, the attractive wooden employee's residence is seen to the left as the trail crosses the road. The permanent buildings of the administration area are passed shortly thereafter, and the Bear Gulch Visitor Center is soon at hand. Be sure to visit it. Publications and exhibits are available, and friendly, knowledgeable park people are on duty to answer any questions.

D. **High Peaks Trail**

Difficulty: Strenuous. Extremely scenic, but only recommended for hikers in reasonably good condition. Avoid the middle of a hot summer day!

Distance: 5.4 miles (8.7 km) from Chalone Creek Picnic Area to Bear Gulch Visitor Center. Several alternative loops are possible. Check map and plan route carefully.

Relief: 1,580 feet, with up-and-down stretches, or 1,330 feet starting at the Bear Gulch Trailhead.

Physically, this can be a strenuous climb, but the higher reaches are very scenic and exciting and lead the hiker into a close intimacy with the imposing rock spires of the high peaks.

Take water and leave the trailhead adjacent to the Chalone Creek picnic area on a climb that starts immediately. The trail, steep but well-graded, at first climbs through abundant chaparral cover consisting principally of chamise, manzanita and buckbrush (ceanothus).

Instead of watching your boots move one by one, turn and catch a few glimpses down into the Chalone Creek Valley, the ancient trace of the Chalone Creek fault. Look beyond to the northeast and east at the broadening blue-gray mountainous horizon. A few miles away across the San Andreas fault valley and the San Benito River, the high hills fade in the hazy distance.

At switchbacks, note outcrops of hardened volcanic ash (tuffaceous andesitic material). Some have a dull, glassy appearance and are called *perlite*. Within the first mile, watch for the coarse blue-green foliage of a California juniper.

Above the third major switchback, the trail levels out a bit and ascends south and west through a stretch of the woodland-savannah community of pretty grasslands dotted with small blue oaks. Many deer may be seen here in early morning and late evening.

Glimpses of the high peaks are becoming more frequent and closer as the trail tops a small rise with a fine rocky view ahead. At 2.1 miles is the junction with the Condor Gulch Trail to the visitor center. This route down, for those not wishing to ascend higher, is 1.7 miles long. The fun, however, still lies ahead.

In less than 0.5 mile, the trail enters the rocky and fascinating maze of the pinnacles, topped by Hawkins Peak at 2,720 feet. The route now undulates over minor rocky crests to the junction with the Tunnel Trail, which connects with the Juniper Canyon Trail leading down to the Chaparral area, 1.8 miles below. A few minutes later on a ridgecrest on the High Peaks Trail, look down to the Chaparral visitor area and beyond to the Gabilan range.

Continue to the base of a steep cliff, which is ascended safely up a staircase hewed into the rock by imaginative workers before World War II. A hand rail is provided to safeguard the short climb. Watch your step as the trail winds through the rock over another spectacular section, again safeguarded by rails attached to iron pipes drilled into the rock. The trail goes over another sharp ridgecrest at about 2,600 feet elevation before winding down to its junction with the Juniper Canyon Trail. Here is located a rock restroom and a bench on which to sit and enjoy the expansive views.

Now the High Peaks Trail drops rapidly down the steep, rocky hillside toward the visitor center less than 2.0 miles away. It switchbacks and passes through a tunnel 0.5 mile from the Juniper Canyon Trail junction, then continues down a long ridge through chaparral vegetation with fine views of the North Chalone Peak lookout and the spires surrounding the reservoir. About 0.5 mile below the tunnel, watch for the rock spire on the right that resembles a howling wolf with its nose to the sky. A few minutes later, the Rim Trail, which leads 0.4 mile to the reservoir, swings off to the right.

Green vegetation is starting to appear, and coast live oaks tower above the trail.

In a short distance, the unsigned Wall Trail, for climbers access only, leads off to the right. Now the route winds down a series of short, steep switchbacks amongst large rocks. During several months of the year, the sound of running water from Bear Creek gurgles from deep within the rocks. A few feet beyond, the trail passes coast live oaks, toyon and a California buckeye, until merging with the Moses Spring Trail.

The final 0.2 mile leads to the Moses Spring Trailhead parking lot. Continue through the picnic area to reach the visitor center and administration area.

E. **North Wilderness Trail**

Difficulty: Strenuous. Very scenic, but only recommended for hikers with off-trail experience. No major trail construction, bridges or elaborate signs will be found, although irregularly-spaced metal fence pickets do mark the way. This route is meant to lead the hiker into a wilderness experience. A topographical map and a compass should be part of the day's equipment, along with water and food.

Distance: The Wilderness Trail itself embraces about 7.6 miles (12.2 km). As a complete loop to Chaparral Picnic Area and return via Balconies and Old Pinnacles Trails to the starting point at the Chalone Creek Trailhead, the distance is approximately 12.3 miles (19.8 km) or 11.9 miles using the cave route. Some will wish to make this trek in the reverse direction from the Chaparral area.

Relief: About 1,277 feet from the trailhead. The trail climbs and undulates over steep chaparral-covered ridges after leaving the North Fork of Chalone Creek.

Take the Old Pinnacles Trail along Chalone Creek about 1.0 mile to the North Fork of Chalone Creek. From here, the unimproved Wilderness Trail leads north and west in a gentle climb up the creek valley. All distances on it will be given from this point. The route, which begins on the west side of the creek, features typical stream valley plants, with cottonwoods, willows, California live and valley oaks and sycamore predominating.

Several stream fordings are made but only in the late winter and spring can these present any difficulties and then only at the expense of wet feet.

This is a pretty valley, in which the gentle chaparral-covered ridges above contrast with the trees and small grassy meadows in the creek bottom. The only real evidence that man has been here is the remains of an old homestead near Willow Spring, about 0.5 mile from the junction with Old Pinnacles Trail. California junipers contrast with the other plants and miner's lettuce is prominent as a distinctive (and edible) ground cover.

Beyond the Willow Spring run-off, the valley widens and flattens. At 1.3 miles, a steep stream valley enters from the left. Up this canyon, note the striking mass of gray rhyolite that resembles a huge elephant with its right side toward the viewer. At 1.5 miles, another intermittent tributary stream enters directly from the north.

It is relatively easy traveling up the pretty valley as the trail swings in a westerly direction at an elevation of 1,400 feet. Here, about 3.6 miles from the Old Pinnacles junction, the trail abruptly leaves the main creek, which continues up a rocky valley to the west and beyond the monument boundary.

Turning directly south, the trail now follows a steeper and narrower stream course to about 5.5 miles and an elevation of near 1,600 feet.

At this point, the trail leaves the small valley and climbs steeply 0.5 mile up a chaparral-covered hillside to its highest point at the top of a prominent ridge at about 2,290 feet. Fine views of the rugged mountainous terrain are seen. To the south and east, the serrated rocky mass of the high peaks and Machete Ridge present an awesome view, while beyond is seen the North Chalone Peak and its lookout. Closer and below but still over two miles away is the Chaparral area, with a ranger station, campground and restrooms.

The trail now alternately ascends and descends some minor steep ridges crisscrossed with old range cattle trails and dozer lines until it finally descends into the watercourse that leads to Chaparral. On a warm day, the cold drinking water at the restroom tastes particularly good.

From here, it's an easy return to the Chalone Creek Trailhead via the wide Balconies and Old Pinnacles Trails (at 3.3 miles if through the caves).

The Wilderness Trail is at its best in the spring when vegetation is green and the wildflowers are on display.

F.   **South Chalone Creek Valley Route**

Difficulty: Easy except for the minor problems associated with route finding and keeping feet dry crossing the creek. Be sure to carry water. A topographical map may help.

Distance: Six miles (9.6 km) roundtrip from Highway 146 adjacent to the Bench Trail.

Relief: About 160 feet.

This pleasant journey on an easy but unmaintained trail is recommended during the spring months of March and April, when the valley floor and adjacent hillsides are ablaze with wildflowers and new

A huge valley oak, the largest species of the oak family, provides welcome summer shade near the Bench Trail and the beginning of the Chalone Creek Valley Route.

vegetation. The fall months of October and November, when the summer heat has passed and the autumn colors are on display, are other times worthy of this valley trek. This "trace" trail hike of about 3.0 miles to the connection with the wilderness climb to South Chalone Peak (Section II-F) can be taken any time of the year, however, except when Chalone Creek is very high. Check at the visitor center.

Leave the Bench Trail at 0.6 mile from the Pinnacles Campground, where a narrow dirt road heads south. Lovely huge valley and coast live oaks shade the hiker as the road is followed for slightly more than 1,000 feet, where it dips into a distinct hollow. Look for a metal fence picket near a large gray pine about 50 feet from the road on the right (west) side. These metal pickets, at irregular intervals, will mark the trail for its entire length.

A few minutes walking across a pretty partially tree-shaded meadow will lead to the first crossing of Chalone Creek, which, although nearly waterless during the summer months, can become a small river in the winter and into spring. As no bridges exist, soaked boots can face the hiker on these crossings. Following this first crossing, the trail will meander south on the flat benches above Chalone Creek on the west side for almost 1.5 miles.

Large Fremont cottonwood trees, sycamores, live oaks and gray pines mark the meandering course of Chalone Creek, while the riotous spring colors, including lupine and California poppies, are a delight around every bend.

Watch for poison oak, which thrives in the valley in its three forms as a prostrate three-leaved plant, as a tall shrub and as a climbing vine. Its fall reddish color is magnificent, but refrain from bouquets!

At about 1.0 mile, the high, rounded and chaparral-covered peak to the west and high above is Mt. Defiance, at 2,657 feet. A fence with a narrow gate is encountered at about 1.5 miles. Be sure to close it behind you. Ahead, a steep slope ends the easy travel and a second creek crossing to the east bank is advised. Don't dry your boots, however, for in about 1,000 feet, a barrier hillside forces another creek crossing again to the west side.

A pig/cattle fence has been constructed on or near the monument's east boundary. Cattle can move into the park at the end of the fence (located at the Section 13-Section 24 interface on the topographic map) but are unlikely to be nearby because of the topography. At about 0.5 mile further, a fourth crossing allows easier travel on the east bench.

The southern 0.5 mile of the trail remains on the east side (outside) of the fence. The park boundary is indefinite in this area, with Chalone Creek proper flowing outside the park. Rungs have been placed on a fence panel to facilitate its crossing.

Rough, narrow trails of range cattle crisscross the hillsides. Feral pigs may be encountered in spite of the fence, but are shy and elusive and will run when people approach. These pigs have descended from escaped domestic pigs, and possibly have interbred with the non-native Russian wild boar, which were introduced to Monterey County many years ago for hunting purposes.

Deer are frequently spotted and birdlife is prolific, with the large, soaring form of the turkey vulture commonly observed above the ridgecrests. Watch for wild turkeys, which are often heard and seen along this route.

Jeep trails, occasionally used by local cattle ranchers, are seen here and there on the hillsides outside the monument boundary.

At about 3.0 miles, the "trace" will cross and leave the creek on its west side and begin the climb to the South Chalone Peak up a brushed route through heavy chaparral growth. Looking up, one can see the highest peak of the monument at 3,304 feet, the North Chalone Peak, but the lookout tower cannot be seen from this angle.

This spot is the lowest point, at about 800 feet. For those who began this hike well-prepared for the all-day and strenuous South Wilderness loop (see recommended route in Section II), the hike has only begun. For the visitor who desires only the pleasant Chalone Creek Valley hike, it is time to turn around and admire new vistas that appear as the return up the gentle valley is commenced.

SECTION II - BEAR GULCH VISITOR CENTER AND PARK HEADQUARTERS

A. Moses Spring/Bear Gulch Caves Trail

Degree of Difficulty: Not only easy, but shaded.

Distance: 0.7 mile (1.1 km) on the Moses Spring branch, slightly shorter through the caves. This trail feels longer because of the many interesting attractions.

Relief: 280 feet from the Bear Gulch Trailhead to the reservoir.

The most heavily-used network of trails in the monument is the cluster that serves Moses Spring, the always-popular Bear Gulch Caves and the reservoir area.

This physically easy but thoroughly fascinating journey begins at the limited parking area above the Bear Gulch picnic area. Many arrive at this trailhead on busy spring weekends via the shuttlebus from the overflow parking area near the entrance station or from the Chalone Creek picnic area.

If the trip through the cool, dark and often wet caves is in order, do not fail to provide a good working flashlight for every two persons. A useful and helpful self-guiding trail guide is available at the visitor center.

The climb begins under the foliage of the huge California live oak. It is an evergreen, hence the name. As the ascent continues, the blue oak, California buckeye (Aesculus californica) and toyon (Christmas berry) are passed. The Mexican manzanita, buckbrush (ceanothus) and the chamise (greasewood) are seen above the trail. Various flowers are here to be enjoyed in season, as are the smaller, less noticeable plants. At 0.2 mile, pass the junction with the High Peaks Trail.

Note the long root of a gray pine to the left of the trail. These trees, in a life-long quest for water, have produced roots that have been measured up to 150 feet in length.

The trail passes through a short tunnel constructed prior to World War II. Our parks could not afford work to match this anymore.

Look up to the imposing multi-hued rock walls. In a few minutes, the Moses Spring Trail leads to the right, where it swings above the caves.

Our route now climbs into a rocky but wooded maze where, a few minutes later, the entrance to the caves is at hand. Enjoy this trip. It is unique!

Have the flashlights at the ready and be prepared for some stooping and squeezing. Short sections are completely dark and will twist and turn. Watch for "headache" rocks! Where any deviation from the route might occur, white directional arrows have been painted on the walls. Some water is usually unavoidable and wet feet may result.

Light from above penetrates in several places and often voices of people traveling the overhead Moses Spring Trail will be heard.

Finally, emerge from the dark section to brilliant light before entering a short passage with subdued light, where the flashlights are no longer necessary.

Step out of the narrow rocky defile to the junction with the Moses Spring Trail, which leads left in slightly less than 0.7 mile back to the trailhead. Ahead, a rocky stairway ascends to the lovely little body of water of the reservoir. Do not drink the water, and no swimming is allowed.

Steps carved from solid rock ascend to the reservoir from the Bear Gulch Caves. This was a project of the mid-1930's.

This is a convenient place to relax, perhaps eat a lunch, and contemplate the imposing rocks that tower above. The large dark forms of turkey vultures are usually seen as they effortlessly soar high above the brightly-hued rocks.

Here is the beginning of the Chalone Peak Trail (Section II-E), which leads a rather arduous 3.3 miles to the highest point of the monument at 3,304 feet. The Rim Trail (Section II-B) commences here also, and crosses above the tops of the Moses Spring and Discovery Walls for 0.4 of a mile to its connection with the High Peaks Trail.

The time to return to the trailhead down the enticing Moses Spring Trail is at hand. As the descent of the steps cut into the rock is begun, look up to the right at the large man-hewn rocks that comprise the dam. This again was a project of the C.C.C., to help furnish water for the residents and visitor operations prior to World War II.

Turn right on the Moses Spring Trail at the foot of the steps and follow it down through large boulders and plants, including the elderberry with its five pinnate leaves. A California juniper, with its distinctive blue-gray foliage, is prominent, and gray pines, with their crazily-tilted growth pattern, grace the rocks above. Note the lichens on the otherwise bare rock in many places. They can often be very colorful, with green, orange and red hues.

Where the trail passes above the upper caves, several openings could allow rocks to be dislodged and endanger people below. Please be careful and follow the safety precautions outlined in the self-guiding leaflet.

Voices can often be heard emitting from the caves or from the adjacent walls, where rock climbers can frequently be seen amidst their colorful ropes and slings.

As the trail drops, some imposing walls and monoliths of rock now tower up to 100 feet above.

To the left of the trail, water seeps down through tiny openings in the rock and feeds Moses Spring, which runs in all seasons, even in the driest years. An out-of-print leaflet stated that two homesteaders along Chalone Creek were working on this trail in the 1920's. As the story is told, one of the men saw a damp spot and said, "Moses smote the rock and water came forth. I'll smite this one." A few blows of his pick then opened the spring.

In a few minutes, the lovely opening in the rock to the left, appropriately called Fern Chamber, appears. Enough water usually collects here year-round to nurture a lush group of the long-fronded chain fern (Woodwardia imbricata). If photographs are in order, allow plenty of light for your camera.

Climber-access only spur trails are to be noted, including a prominent one on the left called the Wall Trail. Some access routes must be closed occasionally to allow revegetation.

Views down the rugged gorge of Bear Gulch with its many rocky defiles are photogenic.

Alas, too soon the trail merges with the caves route and the pleasant return through the tunnel is soon completed.

With the help of the self-guiding trail leaflet, a short but memorable journey through this enticing pinnacled area of caves, gray pines and live oaks is terminated at the parking area or further on at the visitor center. Check out its many exhibits, publications and information from knowledgeable and friendly rangers.

B. **Rim Trail**
    Difficulty: Easy.
    Distance: Only 0.4 (0.6 km) mile. Connects the reservoir and the upper end of the Bear Gulch Caves and Moses Spring Trails with the High Peaks Trail.
    Relief: 90 ft.

This short but scenic route passes along the steep rocky hillside that overlooks Bear Gulch and its caves and the Moses Spring Trail.

From the reservoir at about 1,600 feet elevation, the Rim Trail leads directly north. It climbs slightly to 1,690 feet as it passes above some of the short but steep rocks that are frequented by rock climbers, including the Moses Spring and Discovery Walls. **Some paths do lead onto the tops and shoulders of these rocks. Use caution, watch the footing and do not venture too close to the edge of any of these sheer rock walls.** The trail undulates downward the final 0.2 of a mile to its junction with the High Peaks Trail. Continue down it less than 0.5 mile to return to the Bear Gulch Picnic Area.

C. **High Peaks Trail**
    See Section I-D.

D. **Condor Gulch Trail**
    Difficulty: Moderate. A steep and steady climb, but with very interesting geology, plants and scenery.
    Distance: 1.7 miles (2.7 km).
    Relief: 1,060 feet.

The Condor Gulch Trail is used as part of the High Peaks Loop, the second most popular hike on the east side of the park.

This route is also a part of the Pinnacles Geological Trail, with a well-written and illustrated guidebook available at the visitor center to accompany the hiker. The geology hike climbs Condor Gulch to its junction with the High Peaks Trail and then continues down it east to the Chalone Creek Trailhead, for a total distance of 3.8 miles. Ten of the illustrated stations are on the Condor Gulch section.

Stop at the visitor center for a guidebook, then start the hike from the parking area. In just a few feet, a blue oak is seen, as well as a Park Service weather station.

The trail passes through typical chaparral-type vegetation with chamise, buckbrush and manzanita dominating. A large gray pine looms above.

Watch for the rock outcrops mentioned in the guidebook. In places, look back down to the administration area. The trail follows a steep sidehill just above the bottom of the canyon. A large toyon or Christmas berry is seen on the left. A huge eroded boulder of rhyolite also makes its appearance on the left. More toyon, chamise and a small coast live oak are passed. The way continues climbing up into a rocky gorge.

In less than 0.7 of a mile, the first switchback is negotiated. Ahead are large rugged rocks of the dominant volcanic material called rhyolitic breccia that cover about 60 percent of the monument. A gray pine is on the right. At the rocks, the trail turns up and sharply to the left. Several large red-barked manzanitas grow here. In another few hundred feet, an overlook is reached, with some interesting erosional potholes in the underlying rock. In season, the sight and sound of a spectacular waterfall delights the hiker.

Above the potholes, the trail doubles back again as it continues to climb. Across the valley to the southeast, note the banded appearance of a large mass of rhyolite. The route now swings to the northwest as it climbs close to a barren ridgecrest at about one mile. Beyond are views to the east and to the area of the San Andreas fault near the valley of the San Benito River.

The steady climb continues through dry-appearing chaparral to its junction with the High Peaks Trail. Here, on the ridgecrest at 2,300 feet, are fine views of the surrounding country.

This is the end of the Condor Gulch Trail. To the left, the High

Peaks Trail enters the exciting rocky maze and the jagged spires for which it is named, and to the right it drops down another 2.1 miles to the trailhead at Chalone Creek.

If the hiker is well-equipped and feeling fit, a recommended continuation is to turn left through the rocks of the high peaks and back down to the headquarters area. (See High Peaks Trail, Section 1-D.)

E. **Chalone Peak Trail**
   Difficulty: Strenuous. For sweeping views of the monument and the surrounding region, this trail is one of the best.
   Distance: 3.3 miles (5.3 km) to the fire lookout tower from the beginning of the trail at the reservoir. Total distance from the Bear Gulch Trailhead, 4.0 miles (6.4 km). Add 0.3 mile if starting from the visitor center.
   Relief: 1,984 feet from the Bear Gulch Trailhead.

Follow the Moses Spring Trail or travel through the Bear Gulch Caves (Section II-A) after leaving the Bear Gulch Trailhead. Either way, climb the stairs carved out of rock that lead to the dam and reservoir. The Bear Gulch Dam was constructed by the C.C.C. during the mid-1930's.

The Chalone Peak Trail starts at the junction here, and continues to the left around the reservoir, passing holly-leaf cherry and coast live oak as it begins to climb. Visible ahead are five needle-like pinnacles called the Five Sisters.

The trail crosses a rivulet (running in winter and early spring) and enters the Garden of Giants, an area noted for its flowering shrubs and wildflower displays in the spring. Continue to climb through chaparral cover of buckbrush, holly-leaf cherry, chamise, manzanita and toyon. Pause a moment and enjoy the fine view of the high peaks.

Beware the three-leaved poison oak on both sides of the trail at about 0.5 mile. As the trail levels, there are good views to the east of the Little Pinnacles, Mt. Defiance, Frog Canyon and the Diablo Range in the distance and to the west of the high peaks.

Continue up past an impressive rock outcrop. As the ascent steepens, the chaparral-covered North and South Chalone Peaks come into view. With each step upward, the views become more impressive.

As the climb continues, note the California juniper on the right. To the east can be seen the San Andreas fault zone that runs near the San Benito River valley a few miles from the monument's eastern boundary.

Views to the west of the Salinas Valley and the Santa Lucia Range open up near a large blue oak that reaches over the trail.

At 2.4 miles, the trail widens as it bears left uphill at the signed junction. In a short distance the trail joins the narrow road that ascends steeply to the fire lookout.

North Chalone Peak at 3,304 feet is the highest point in the monument. The 360° panorama from the summit rivals any in Pinnacles. It includes the Salinas Valley and the meandering Salinas River, virtually all of the monument, the distant mountain ranges to the east and west, and on a clear day, the Pacific Ocean.

A restroom is located just below the summit on the east side of the peak.

After enjoying the view, you have the option of retracing your steps or, if experienced in crosscountry travel, continuing another 1.6 miles to South Chalone Peak and beyond on the South Wilderness Trail.

F.   **South Wilderness Trail**

This route is subject to change. Please check with park rangers before attempting this trail.

Difficulty: Extremely strenuous — very scenic. Recommended for those with cross-country hiking experience. No standard trail signs, major trail construction or bridges will be found. Carry a topographic map and compass. Plan to start early.

Distance: The Wilderness Trail itself, connecting the Chalone Peak Trail with the South Chalone Creek Valley Route, is approximately 3.6 miles (5.8 km). However, if you desire to complete the loop from the visitor center, up the Chalone Peak Trail, and then down and out to Highway 146 at the Bench Trail, the total distance is approximately 10.5 miles (16.8 km.)

Relief: Because of two strenuous ascents and descents, a total elevation gain from the Bear Gulch Trailhead of 2,655 ft., and a loss of 2,920 ft. to Highway 146.

For hikers who wish to complete the Wilderness Trail combined with the Chalone Peak Trail and the South Chalone Creek Valley Route as a spectacular day-long high loop, the recommended way is from the Bear Gulch Trailhead. Hike to the reservoir and join the Chalone Peak Trail (Section II-E).

The CCC laid out a trail from North to South Chalone Peak and had started the construction when the project was canceled by World

War II in 1942. Some work was done, even some stonework completed, and it is still possible to find a stray survey stake outlining the route to South Chalone Peak.

The route leaves the Chalone Peak Trail about 300 yards below the lookout on the summit of North Chalone Peak and descends moderately for 0.6 miles through areas of dense chaparral to the saddle between North and South Chalone Peaks. It is easy to see how the heavy chaparral cover kept this trail "undiscovered" for many years. From the saddle one has good views of the exposed slabs of fine-textured rhyolite near the head of the Frog Canyon drainage, and of the Salinas Valley. Frog Canyon was the route originally proposed for the South Wilderness Trail, but was abandoned because it would have involved extensive construction.

The trail climbs from the saddle through chaparral for another 0.6 mile to South Chalone Peak at 1.2 miles. California juniper and gray pine begin to appear near the top of the peak. The vistas from South Chalone's rocky summit more than make up for the climb from the saddle, with the view of North Chalone Peak from the southeast being perhaps the most spectacular. This side of the peak is precipitous and rocky. After absorbing the panorama, begin the steep descent. The chaparral-covered Mt. Defiance is visible to the north. Gray pines cover the hillside to the northeast.

Much of the trail ahead is brushed over and very hard to negotiate. The route heads east down the open ridge, traversing grassy knolls and passing some rock outcrops. At about 1,800 feet elevation, the route bears northeast and drops about 1,000 feet through chaparral. Two intermittent side streams are crossed before the trail meets Chalone Creek at 3.6 miles.

The three relatively easy miles up the pretty valley of South Chalone Creek will bring the hiker to the junction of the Bench Trail adjacent to Highway 146, only 0.6 miles from the campground.

SECTION III – CHAPARRAL TRAILHEAD – WEST SIDE

A. Balconies Cliff and Balconies Caves Trail

Difficulty: Moderate. Short but extremely scenic. This is a self-guiding nature trail. Pick up the descriptive leaflet at the ranger station before beginning.

Distance: The Balconies Cliff Trail is 1.4 miles (2.2 km) and the route through the caves is approximately 1.0 mile (1.6 km). A loop along the base of the Balconies cliffs to the junction with Old Pinnacles Trail and a return through the caves is a highly recommended 2.4 mile (3.9 km) hike. Be sure to carry flashlights if you contemplate choosing the cave option.

Relief: 360 feet along the Balconies cliffs. Approximately 200 feet through the caves. The low point of 1,240 ft. is reached at the junction of Balconies Trail and Old Pinnacles.

For those who wish to experience an intimacy with the Pinnacles scenery with as little hiking as possible, the Balconies Trail has no peer in the monument. From the rocky, rugged little gorge to the soaring, near vertical cliffs of the Balconies and Machete Ridge, the scenery is impressive and exciting. The trip through the caves is a

The Balconies from the High Peaks Trail. The chaparral-clothed Gabilan Range looms in the background.

great adventure for young and old. Rock climbers sporting colorful gear are often seen and heard only a short distance above the trail. This small area is often referred to as "Little Yosemite."

From the trailhead at Chaparral, follow the well-traveled broad trail northeast toward the Machete Ridge rocks looming in the near distance. A sign informs the hiker that this trail leads 3.3 miles to the eastside trailhead at Chalone Creek Picnic Area.

A car pickup at the opposite end of this trail, however, requires lengthy and difficult arrangements. It is best to plan on returning to your starting point. Other routes involve much more difficult ascents. Check your guide or a topographical map carefully.

For the first 0.5 mile, the trail is broad and easy and actually drops slightly. Large gray pines frame the rocks ahead. Passing amongst some huge boulders, the trail drops into the cool, shaded creek bottom and soon an attractive footbridge is reached. The longer trail along the Balconies cliffs crosses the bridge, while the narrower trail to the caves is straight ahead. As a loop, the 2.4 mile trip is highly recommended, with the trail along the cliffs preferred as the first leg. The climb is gentler in this direction, and the route through the caves easier to find from east to west.

A hiker on the delightful Balconies Trail leading from the Chaparral visitor area on the west side of the monument. The Machete Ridge looms ahead.

Do not attempt to enter the caves during periods of high water in the winter and early spring and be sure to have at least one adequate flashlight for every two people.

This is a lovely little canyon, shaded by a variety of large water-loving trees and the high rocks above. Savor this short hike on a hot summer day. Whichever trail is followed, the last portion will be downhill to the Old Pinnacles Trail junction.

This is a short but memorable hike for family groups, and no special equipment is needed but a flashlight or two.

B. **Juniper Canyon Trail**
    Difficulty: Strenuous.
    Distance: 1.8 miles (2.9 km) from Chaparral Trailhead to the junction with the High Peaks Trail at the ridgecrest.
    Relief: 1,100 feet to the High Peaks junction.

The Juniper Canyon Trail is perhaps the most scenic trip in the monument when combined with a loop on the Tunnel Trail and a portion of the High Peaks Trail. Study alternative loops and possible objectives carefully. Any further hiking other than a direct return to Chaparral will add considerable distance and time.

Leave the Chaparral Trailhead for an exciting day among the jagged and imposing rock spires that tower over 1,000 feet above. A large California juniper rears its gray-green foliage to the right as the trail ascends very gradually along an intermittent stream that appears to be dry most of the year.

Some small blue oaks, coast live oaks and more junipers are passed, thriving in this rocky and dry habitat. When more water is present in the spring, the wildflower display, highlighted by the golden-orange of the California poppy, can be gorgeous.

At about 0.3 mile, the trail steepens as it enters Juniper Canyon just above the creek. Toyon, holly-leaved cherry and poison oak dot the hillsides above and below the trail. As the trail winds closer to the high rocks, some sheer walls tower not far above the trail. Take note of the obvious banded appearance of the rocks in which the bands dip steeply toward the west. These represent different lava flows, one on top of another, formed over a period of thousands or millions of years. Many years of physical erosion by running water and wind-driven sand occurred between flows. Each band, therefore, represents an uncomfortable contact in geological terms.

At about 0.7 mile, the trail enters the upper part of the canyon, where it is quite shaded by very abundant and pleasant vegetation including the blue oak, coast live oak, holly-leaved cherry and gray pine. Even in the fall, pools of water usually are found in portions of the creekbed. This is Oak Tree Spring.

The imposing walls of rhyolitic breccia now loom close above the trail, which switchbacks up a broad, relatively treeless ridgecrest. The campground and ranger station are in view below, and to the west beyond the Salinas Valley, the distant hazy blue range of the Santa Lucia uplift looms on the horizon. Several big-berried manzanitas grow above the trail. Deer trails crisscross the slopes below, while some gray pines are growing out of the cracks in the rocks at crazy tilted angles.

At 1.2 miles, the junction with the Tunnel Trail is reached (Section III-C) at an altitude of 2,280 feet.

Six-tenths of a mile and 200 vertical feet later, the high ridgecrest is topped at 2,500 ft. elevation and 1.8 miles total distance from Chaparral. Enjoy the great views. Directly below to the southeast, the High Peaks Trail is seen meandering down through chaparral and along steep rock ridgecrests as it drops to Bear Gulch in less than two steep miles. To the west across a near broad valley, the lower chaparral-covered peaks of the Gabilan Range form the horizon.

A stone restroom and a bench offer the hiker some of the amenities of home. This is the end of the Juniper Canyon Trail. If time and energy permit, the recommendation is to turn north on the High Peaks Trail as it twists and turns in a spectacular fashion through the rocky maze of spires and walls, including Hawkins Peak, that loom above. (See Section I-D).

If you take this route, enjoy the exciting half-mile or so to the next junction, which is with the Tunnel Trail. Turn left (southwest) through the rocks down a series of steep switchbacks, through the long cool tunnel and across a steep rocky gorge on a high concrete bridge built long before World War II. Rejoin the Juniper Canyon Trail down to Chaparral and look back on a memorable day and a great hike.

C. Tunnel Trail

Difficulty: Easy if hiked downhill from junction with High Peaks Trail. Moderate if hiked uphill from the junction with the Juniper Canyon Trail.

Distance: 0.6 mile (1 km)

Relief: 260 feet

This trail is really only a short spur that links the High Peaks Trail at the upper end with the Juniper Canyon Trail at the lower end. The long tunnel bored through the solid rock is very interesting and the attractive concrete bridge high above a steep rocky gorge is well worth a short detour from the Juniper Canyon Trail.

After leaving the junction with the High Peaks Trail, 19 very short sharp switchbacks lose altitude rapidly as the trail winds down through some rocks. Very soon, the entrance to the tunnel is reached. Following the cool trip through it (106 feet), the bridge is crossed and, shortly thereafter, the meeting with the Juniper Canyon Trail is made.

D. **North Wilderness Trail**

See Section I-E for description.

REFERENCES

Anon., BALCONIES SELF-GUIDING TRAIL, Southwest Parks and Monuments Association, revised 1993.

___, CHECKLIST OF AMPHIBIANS, REPTILES, and MAMMALS, PINNACLES NATIONAL MONUMENT.

___, CHECKLIST OF BIRDS, PINNACLES NATIONAL MONUMENT.

___, FLORA OF PINNACLES NATIONAL MONUMENT.

___, MOSES SPRING SELF-GUIDING TRAIL, Pinnacles National Monument, 1993.

___, PINNACLES OFFICIAL MAP AND GUIDE, National Park Service, U.S. Dept. of the Interior.

___, PINNACLES NATIONAL MONUMENT, TOPOGRAPHICAL MAP, U.S.G.S., 1969.

Head, W.S., THE CALIFORNIA CHAPARRAL, AN ELFIN FOREST. Naturegraph Publishers, Inc., Healdsburg, CA, 1972.

Keith, Sandra L., PINNACLES NATIONAL MONUMENT, Southwest Parks and Monuments Association, Tucson, AZ, 1991.

Kroeber, A.L., HANDBOOK OF THE INDIANS OF CALIFORNIA. California Book Co., Ltd., Berkeley, 1953.

Matthews, Vincent and Webb, Ralph C., PINNACLES GEOLOGICAL TRAIL, Southwest Parks and Monuments Associaion, 1982.

Matthews, Vincent, GEOLOGY OF PINNACLES NATIONAL MONUMENT, Unpublished Dissertation, University of California, Santa Cruz.

Moore, Chad, PICTORIAL MAP, PINNACLES NATIONAL MONUMENT, 1993.

Oberg, Rita, THE ADMINISTRATIVE HISTORY OF PINNACLES NATIONAL MONUMENT (unpublished), 1979.

Rubine, Dave, CLIMBER'S GUIDE – PINNACLES NATIONAL MONUMENT, Chalkstone Press, Evergreen, CO, 1991.

Webb, Ralph C., A GUIDE TO THE PLANTS OF THE PINNACLES, Southwest Parks and Monuments Association, 1971.

___, NATURAL HISTORY OF THE PINNACLES NATIONAL MONUMENT, Pinnacles Natural History Association, 1969.

INDEX